12 INSECTS
BACK FROM THE BRINK

by Samantha S. Bell

12 STORY LIBRARY

www.12StoryLibrary.com

12-Story Library is an imprint of Peterson Publishing Company and Press Room Editions.

Produced for 12-Story Library by Red Line Editorial

Photographs ©: Al Behrman/AP Images, cover, 1; Jean-Pierre Boudot/IUCN, 4; US Fish and Wildlife Service, 6, 7; Igor Golovniov/Shutterstock Images, 8; Debbie Oetgen/Shutterstock Images, 9; Animals Animals/SuperStock, 10; Shutterstock Images, 11, 12, 15, 18, 25, 28, 29; Henrik Larson/Shutterstock Images, 13; Marek Velechovsky/Shutterstock Images, 14; Rohan Cleave/Zoos Victoria, 16, 17; Doug Meek/Shutterstock Images, 19; Paul Burton, 20, 21; Craig Slawson, 22; Stuart Connop, 23; Taina Sohlman/Shutterstock Images, 24; Maxine Livingston/Shutterstock Images, 26; Jillian Cain/Shutterstock Images, 27

ISBN
978-1-63235-002-2 (hardcover)
978-1-63235-062-6 (paperback)
978-1-62143-043-8 (hosted ebook)

Library of Congress Control Number: 2014937257

Printed in the United States of America
Mankato, MN
June, 2014

Go beyond the book. Get free, up-to-date content on this topic at 12StoryLibrary.com.

TABLE OF CONTENTS

RENEWED WATER SOURCES HELP CAPE BLUET DAMSELFLY

Cape bluet damselflies may look fragile, but they are hunters. These insects eat any kind of prey they can catch and digest. Their legs form a basket that can scoop other insects right out of the air. But a water shortage in South Africa threatened their survival.

The damselflies lived near streams and other wetlands in South Africa.

Cape bluet damselflies are recognizable by their purplish color.

IUCN RED LIST

The International Union for the Conservation of Nature (IUCN) keeps a list of all threatened species in the world, called the Red List. Each species is labeled according to how at risk it is.

Least Concern: Not considered at risk.

Near Threatened: At risk of being vulnerable or endangered in the future.

Vulnerable: At risk of extinction.

Endangered: At high risk of extinction.

Critically Endangered: At extremely high risk of extinction.

Extinct in the Wild: Only lives in captivity.

Extinct: No members of a species are left.

They laid their eggs in the water. Their larvae grew there, too. But humans in the area also needed water. The government used canals to move the water to areas where people needed it. Farmers planted trees that also used a lot of water. The streams began drying up. The cape bluet damselfly was last seen in 1962. Scientists thought the species was extinct.

The South African government decided to do something about the water shortage. It partnered with communities to clear away plants and trees that had been using up the water. The streams returned. Sunlight could reach the pools, and water plants grew again. In 2003, people started seeing the damselflies again. Scientists do not know where they had been hiding all those years, but they were not extinct after all.

41
Years the cape bluet damselfly survived without being seen.

Status: Critically endangered
Population: Fewer than 50
Home: South Africa
Life Span: Unknown

NORTHEASTERN BEACH TIGER BEETLE BACK ON THE BEACH

The northeastern beach tiger beetle was named for the aggressive way it stalks its prey. It eats flies, sand fleas, spiders, and dead fish. The larvae sometimes even eat each other. These beetles catch their food on the wide, sandy beaches where they live. They used to be found all along the Atlantic coast, from Massachusetts to Virginia. Then the beaches began to disappear.

The beetles lay their eggs in shallow burrows in the soft sand. The larvae live in the burrows for approximately two years. But people use the beaches, too. Visitors drove four-wheelers and other vehicles on the sand. The vehicles crushed the burrows. Residents also built homes on the shore. They built barriers to keep the waves from coming too close. The beaches

Northeastern beach tiger beetles are about the length of a fingernail.

Their pale coloring helps these beetles blend into the sand.

became too hard and narrow. By 1989, only 14 colonies of tiger beetles could be found in Virginia and Maryland.

Conservationists went to work. In 1994, scientists relocated some of the beetles to a wildlife refuge in New Jersey. In 2010, government officials began working with homeowners in Virginia to create offshore barriers. These protect both the homes and beaches. In 2013, the beetles were found at more than 50 sites near Chesapeake Bay.

THINK ABOUT IT

If you lived near one of these beaches with the tiger beetle, would you try to save it? What if protecting the beetle meant that your home could be in danger?

14

Depth in inches (35.6 cm) that tiger beetle larvae will burrow into the sand.

Status: Threatened
Population: More than 10,500
Home: Northeastern US coast
Life Span: Two years

3

TUSKED WETAS RETURN TO ISLANDS

When someone mentions tusks, you probably don't think of a cricket. But the male Middle Island tusked weta is a cricket with tusks. It uses them to butt and push away rivals. Like other crickets, tusked weta have powerful back legs. Some can jump up to almost three feet (1 m).

People first saw the wetas on Middle Island off the coast of New Zealand in 1970. Scientists believe they used to live on other nearby islands, too. Then rats came to the islands on ships. The rats infested the islands and ate the wetas. The wetas

Tusked wetas eat mainly worms and insects.

2.75

Length in inches
(7 cm) of an adult
tusked weta.

Status: Critically
endangered
Population: Unknown
Home: Mercury Islands,
New Zealand
Life Span: 2–4 years

45¢

NE   ND

The tusked weta
was featured on
a New Zealand
stamp to raise
awareness.

survived on Middle Island because it had not been infested with rats.

Scientists wanted the wetas to live on other islands, too, to give them a better chance of survival. In the early 1990s, scientists used poisoned bait to get rid of the rats. The islands were ready just in time. By 1993, scientists could find only five wetas on Middle Island. They caught three of them and started a breeding program. By 2003, almost 150 had been released on two more islands. In 2005, scientists found young wetas in the areas they had been released. That meant that wetas were breeding in the wild.

PREDATORS

Wetas have natural predators on the islands. Birds, reptiles, and bats eat wetas. But they don't eat very many because wetas aren't easy to find. During the day, they stay underground. They come out only on dark nights when the moon isn't shining.

WILDFLOWERS BRING BACK KARNER BLUE BUTTERFLY

Karner blue butterflies lay up to 150 eggs at a time. The caterpillars only eat lupine, a type of wildflower. So when the lupines began to disappear, the butterflies did, too.

Karner blues used to be found in 12 states and in parts of Canada. But over the past 100 years, much of the land was cleared for farming and development. The pines, shrubs, and prairie flowers gave way to roads, buildings, and houses. By 1992, the number of Karner blue butterflies was down by at least 99 percent.

Many groups worked to save this butterfly. In 2000, students in New Hampshire raised lupines

Karner blue butterflies are active for four months out of the year, during the time the lupines are in bloom.

GOOD FOR ALL

When the habitat was restored, the Karner blue butterfly could live there again. So could a lot of other animals that had left. Birds such as Kirtland's warbler returned. So did the slender glass lizard and the wood turtle. Even rattlesnakes came back. The habitat could support all these animals again.

and planted them in the spring. In Wisconsin, a power company started letting the grass grow tall under power lines. The highway department also started leaving grassy areas along roads for lupines to grow. Officials burned overgrown areas so the grassy, open land would return. Scientists raised thousands of butterflies to release in New York, New Hampshire, and Minnesota. In 10 years, more than 13,000 had been released in New York alone. The number of Karner blues continues to increase as their habitat is restored.

7
Number of US states where the Karner blue butterfly lives.

Status: Endangered
Population: More than 100,000
Home: Midwest, Eastern United States
Life Span: 6–8 weeks

Karner blue butterflies are small, with a wingspan of approximately one inch (2.5 cm).

AMERICAN BURYING BEETLE BACK ON CLEANUP DUTY

American burying beetles have an important job. They help clean up dead animals. First, a beetle and its mate pull off all the fur or feathers. Then they roll the meat up into a ball. The beetles bury the "meatball" for later use. This role made them an important part of the ecosystem. But then they started dying off.

The beetles used to live in 35 US states and parts of Canada. By 1989, scientists could find only one group of beetles in Rhode Island. No one was sure what happened to the rest.

American burying beetles are dark-colored with bright red markings.

American burying beetles use their large antennas to detect animal carcasses.

In 1994, scientists collected beetles to breed. A Rhode Island zoo raised more than 5,000 beetles. They put more than 2,800 back into the wild. Two more zoos started raising beetles. As of 2013, the beetles were living in at least five other states.

2

Miles (3.2 km) away a burying beetle can detect a decaying animal using its antennas.

Status: Critically endangered
Population: More than 1,000
Home: United States and Canada
Life Span: Approximately one year

BEETLE PARENTS

American burying beetles take care of their young. After the larvae hatch, the parents feed them from the meatball. The beetles pull off pieces of meat and chew them up. Then they spit them out again for the larvae to eat. They even call their larvae for mealtime by making a squeaking sound.

FIELD CRICKETS SINGING AGAIN IN GREAT BRITAIN

Before it eats, the field cricket has to warm up. In the spring, it's often seen sunbathing outside its burrow. Male crickets sing to attract a female. Unlike most crickets, field crickets can't fly. So when their habitat shrank, they couldn't leave to find another one.

Field crickets are the most endangered crickets in Great Britain. They need land with short grass and bare ground to lay their eggs. Baby crickets, called nymphs, also burrow in the ground. Over the years, their habitat changed. Farmers did not use the open fields where the crickets lived for grazing their livestock anymore. The land became overgrown. By 1991, only 100 field crickets were left in the country. This last group was found in West Sussex, England.

Conservationists and landowners joined together to fix the habitat. Brambles and young trees were removed. Cattle grazed to make the

Male field crickets make a chirping sound by rubbing their wings together.

12

Weeks it takes for a nymph to grow into a cricket.

Status: Least concern
Population: Unknown
Home: Europe, Western Asia, North Africa
Life Span: Approximately eight weeks

Field crickets eat both plant material and insects.

grass short. Two tree farms were replanted with low-growing plants. More crickets were raised in zoos. Since 1991, more than 14,000 crickets have been released. By 2010, four new cricket colonies were thriving.

THINK ABOUT IT

Field crickets eat plants and insects that are considered weeds or pests. They have many predators, including birds, frogs, toads, and other insects. What do you think happens to the other species in the food chain if field crickets disappear?

LORD HOWE ISLAND STICK INSECT SURVIVES IN HIDING

It's no wonder Lord Howe Island stick insects are sometimes called tree lobsters. They are some of the largest insects in the world. They have strong, heavy bodies. They can grow to almost five inches (13 cm) long. But the stick insects can't fly. So when rats invaded their habitat, they didn't have much of a chance.

The insects used to be found all around Lord Howe Island. The island is between Australia and New Zealand. Then in 1918, a ship with rats on it arrived. The rats infested the island and ate the stick insects. By 1920, no more could be found. Forty years later, they were declared extinct.

Nymphs are green. They start to darken in color at around a few months of age.

Lord Howe Island stick insects are the world's heaviest flightless insect.

5

Length in inches (12.7 cm) of a Lord Howe Island stick insect.

Status: Critically Endangered
Population: 20–30 in the wild
Home: Lord Howe Island, Australia
Life Span: 12–18 months

that juts out of the ocean. In 2001, scientists searched Ball's Pyramid for the stick insects. They found 24 of them, and some were taken to zoos to breed. Now thousands are in captivity. Scientists are working on getting rid of the rats on Lord Howe Island. Then the stick insects can be released on the island again.

Near the island is Ball's Pyramid. It's actually the top of a volcano

TRUE SURVIVORS

Scientists aren't sure how the insects got to Ball's Pyramid. They might have been carried by a bird. Perhaps they came over on a piece of fish bait. Most of Ball's Pyramid is steep rocks and cliffs. The insects lived on a single bush. They stayed under the soil during the day and came out on the bush at night. The bush provided food for the insects and soft soil for their eggs.

PRISONERS SAVE TAYLOR'S CHECKERSPOT BUTTERFLY

The caterpillars of the Taylor's checkerspot butterfly spend all winter in cocoons. In the spring, they emerge as medium-sized butterflies. Then they breed, and the females lay up to 1,200 eggs. When settlers started moving west in the 1840s, they probably saw the Taylor's checkerspot butterfly. The butterflies could be found all around the prairies from British Columbia, Canada, to Oregon.

Checkerspot butterflies get their name from the checkered pattern on their wings.

Over the next 150 years, the land was developed. Buildings, roads, and non-native plants replaced the prairies. Pesticides used in farming also hurt the butterflies. By 2009, they could be found in just 15 places in Washington, Oregon, and western Canada.

> Checkerspot butterflies live in grassland and prairie areas with lots of nectar-producing plants.

Help came in an unusual way. A college professor started a project for prisoners at Mission Creek Corrections Center for Women in Washington State. The prisoners studied the butterflies. They identified the butterflies' original host plant and started growing it. Then the prisoners raised hundreds of butterflies. The government bought land to increase the habitat. By 2012, 800 butterflies had been released. In 2013, the butterflies were found at three new sites.

70

Different sites Taylor's checkerspot butterflies used to be found before they lost their habitat.

Status: Endangered
Population: Unknown
Home: Northwestern United States and Canada
Life Span: Approximately one year

THINK ABOUT IT

Sometimes, ordinary people can help a species survive. What do you think students could do to help a species of insects? What could you do in your own yard to create an insect habitat?

HABITATS RESTORED FOR HINE'S EMERALD DRAGONFLY

9

Hine's emerald dragonflies can hover and fly backward. They can fly up to 35 miles per hour (56 km/h). Most of the dragonflies' life is spent in the larva stage. The nymphs live in the water for two to four years. Each one lives for only approximately five weeks as an adult. These are the only endangered dragonflies in the United States.

The dragonflies used to be found throughout the Midwest. Then they began to lose their habitats. The dragonflies lived around spring-fed marshes and meadows. These were drained and filled in for city and business developments. Pesticides polluted the area.

Hine's emerald dragonflies have bright green eyes and a green tint to their bodies.

20,000

Hine's emerald dragonflies estimated to be living in Door County, Wisconsin, two-thirds of the total population.

Status: Near threatened
Population:
   Approximately 30,000
Home: Illinois, Michigan, Missouri, and Wisconsin
Life Span: 2–4 years

Conservationists knew the best way to bring back the dragonflies was to protect their habitat. In 2010, the government set aside national forestland in Michigan and Missouri. The protected habitat went from 13,000 acres (5,261 ha) to 26,000 acres (10,522 ha). Since then, Hine's emerald dragonflies have been showing up in more areas and in greater numbers. Today, a large population lives in Wisconsin.

The Hine's emerald dragonfly has a wingspan of more than three inches (7.6 cm).

STREAKED BOMBARDIER BEETLE GETS NEW HOME

The streaked bombardier beetle can defend itself. It aims at its attacker with its abdomen. Then with a pop, it shoots a bomb of hot, poisonous chemicals. The spray can kill other insects. It can also cause larger predators to leave the beetle alone. But these beetles were not seen in Great Britain for many years. The country listed the species as extinct in 1928.

The beetles lived in dry, sunny areas. They were often found under stones and in chalk quarries. In 2006, they were discovered near the Thames River on brownfield sites. These are places where factories used to

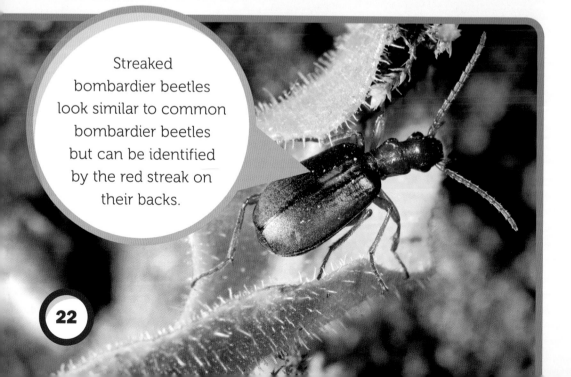

Streaked bombardier beetles look similar to common bombardier beetles but can be identified by the red streak on their backs.

Streaked bombardier beetles feed on other kinds of ground beetles.

be. The thin soil and rubble were just right for the beetles. But new buildings were planned on the sites.

Conservationists, professors, students, and other volunteers wanted to help the beetles. In 2012, they created their own brownfield site at the University of East London. They brought in more than 60 tons (54.4 t) of brick, rubble, and chalk. They also planted wildflowers. The new site was called Beetle Bump. Fifteen beetles were rescued and brought to Beetle Bump. Now the beetles are thriving in their new home.

250
Different kinds of bombardier beetles globally.

Status: Endangered
Population: Unknown
Home: Great Britain
Life Span: Several weeks

READY, AIM, FIRE!

A bombardier beetle is a good shot. It can rotate its abdomen three-fourths of the way around its body. Then it shoots the hot spray. The spray is approximately 212 degrees Fahrenheit (100°C). A beetle can shoot more than 20 times before it uses up its reserves.

HEATH FRITILLARY BUTTERFLIES RETURN TO ENGLAND

In late spring and early summer, heath fritillary butterflies can be seen flying close to the ground. They drink nectar from buttercups, bramble flowers, and daisies. They lay clumps of eggs on the undersides of leaves. After hatching, each caterpillar hibernates, rolled up in a dead leaf. The leaf tube is sealed with silk. The caterpillars emerge the following spring to grow into butterflies. Heath fritillaries used to be common across Europe and Asia. But their population in England declined sharply during the 1900s.

Heath fritillaries thrive in low-growing grassland or heathland areas. The butterflies need

Heath fritillaries are one of the rarest butterflies in England.

The pattern on heath fritillaries' wings varies between butterflies of the same species.

warmth from the sun, so the area can't be overgrown. They often take over a clearing after trees have been cut down. This has earned them the nickname "woodman's follower." But forest clearing became less common in the late 1900s. Land became overgrown, and the butterflies had fewer places to live. In 1980, researchers found 31 colonies in southwest England. By 1995, only 12 small colonies could be found. The United Kingdom listed the species as critically endangered.

Conservationists worked with landowners to create better habitats. They cleared trees and added plants the butterflies need for survival. By 2012, 25 colonies were thriving.

150
Number of eggs a female will lay at a time.

Status: Endangered
Population: Approximately 25 colonies in England
Home: Europe and Asia
Life Span: 6–8 weeks as butterflies

ATALA BUTTERFLIES MAKE A COMEBACK

With their bright colors, atala butterflies and caterpillars are easy to spot. The insects often gather in groups. This makes them even more noticeable. The colors warn predators to stay away. But this didn't help the butterfly when its host plant was gone.

Atala butterflies can't live without coonties, a native Florida plant. The butterflies lay their eggs on the coonties, and the caterpillars eat them. The coontie used to be a food source for people, too. Native Americans and early settlers used the roots to make a wheat substitute. In the early 1800s, people built factories to process the coonties. They made them into biscuits and crackers. Soon, too many plants had been harvested. Development also destroyed the habitat. By 1965, officials thought the atala butterfly was extinct.

Atala butterflies are known for their bright blue and red spots.

Atala caterpillars are orange-red with seven sets of bright yellow spots on their backs.

In 1979, a naturalist discovered a small group of atala butterflies in Florida. Zoos, nature centers, and universities set up research and breeding programs. Thousands of butterflies have been raised. Some are kept in the centers, while others are released. The people in the community are helping as well. Some have been planting coonties in their yards. In 2011, atala butterflies were seen in approximately 130 different locations.

1.5
Width in inches (3.8 cm) of an atala butterfly's wingspan.

Status: Vulnerable
Population: Unknown
Home: Southeast Florida
Life Span: 35–42 days

WARNING: POISON!

Coonties contain a toxin. When the caterpillars eat the coonties, they build up the poison inside. The bright colors of the caterpillars and butterflies warn predators not to eat them. Because the butterflies don't have to escape, they move slowly. They can sometimes even be touched while resting on a flower.

FACT SHEET

- Scientists have found more than 1 million species of insects. Some scientists think Earth may actually have more than 30 million species of insects. Approximately 300,000 of these are types of beetles. There are 8,800 ant species.

- Scientists believe there are approximately 10 quintillion (10,000,000,000,000,000,000) insects on earth at any time.

- Insects are found in almost every kind of habitat. They are an important part of many ecosystems. They provide a food source to many mammals, birds, amphibians, reptiles, and even other insects. Insects are also important for the soil. They break down leaves, wood, and dead organisms.

- Studying insects can give scientists information about the health of an environment. If the insects are gone from an area, it is usually a sign that something is wrong with the air, soil, or water.

- Insects pollinate 75 percent of the world's flowering plants. Bees, wasps, butterflies, beetles, and flies help vegetables and fruits to grow.

- Insects provide people with products like silk, beeswax, and honey. Some people even eat insects. Approximately 500 species of insects are used as food by humans.

- Less than 5 percent of insects are harmful to people. Many of them contain substances that are helpful. Insects are used in scientific and medical research.

- Many countries have laws protecting endangered species. In 1973, the US Congress passed the Endangered Species Act. It requires state and federal government agencies to monitor and protect species that might become extinct. It also bans people from hunting, catching, trading, or possessing animals and plants that are protected.

GLOSSARY

abdomen
The back part of the body of an insect.

conservationist
A person who works to save natural resources.

ecosystem
A system made up of living things that interact with each other.

endangered
Threatened with extinction.

extinct
The death of all members of a species.

habitat
The place where a plant or animal naturally lives or grows.

host plant
The plant a caterpillar feeds on.

larvae
A young insect that is often worm-like.

nymph
An insect that is not fully grown.

pesticide
A chemical used to kill insects and other pests.

predator
An animal that kills or eats another animal.

prey
An animal that is killed or eaten by another animal.

species
A group of animals or plants that are similar and can produce young.

toxin
Poison.

FOR MORE INFORMATION

Books

Boothroyd, Jennifer. *Endangered and Extinct Invertebrates.* Minneapolis: Lerner Publishing Group, 2014.

Burns, Loree Griffin. *Beetle Busters.* Boston: HMH Books, 2014.

Gray, Susan H. *Karner Blue Butterfly.* Ann Arbor, MI: Cherry Lake Publishing, 2014.

Green, Jen. *Incredible Insects: An Amazing Insight Into the Lives of Ants, Termites, Bees and Wasps, Shown in More Than 220 Close-Up Images.* San Francisco: Armadillo, 2014.

Johnson, Robin, and Bobbie Kalman. *Endangered Butterflies.* New York: Crabtree Publishing, 2006.

Kalman, Bobbie, and Kathryn Smithyman. *Insects in Danger.* New York: Crabtree Publishing, 2006.

Websites

National Geographic Kids: Bugs
kids.nationalgeographic.com/kids/photos/bugs

San Diego Zoo Kids: Insects
kids.sandiegozoo.org/animals/insects

US Fish and Wildlife Service: Endangered Species for Kids
www.fws.gov/endangered/education

INDEX

About the Author

Samantha Bell is a graduate of Furman University and has taught writing and art to both children and adults. She has written or illustrated more than 20 books for children.